OUR CALLING
AND
ELECTION

OUR CALLING
AND
ELECTION

Michael Hagen

XULON PRESS

Xulon Press
2301 Lucien Way #415
Maitland, FL 32751
407.339.4217
www.xulonpress.com

Paperback ISBN-13: 978-1-66286-990-7

1

WHO DOES GOD SAY THAT I AM?

* God says we are His Chosen,

* God says we are His Masterpiece,

* God says we are His Adopted Children,

* God says that we are the restored remnant'.

* God says each one of His Children will be made complete, filled with His Holy Wisdom.

* God says we (His Chosen) have worth and value.

* God says He will "bless" us; (His Chosen), with Spiritual gifts beforehand for each one of us!

* God says that we will be made complete.

* God says that we will become a new creation.

* God says that we are "Forgiven" .and now " Blameless".

If...We do our parts, let's consider a few passages.
2nd Peter 1:1-10 v3` For His divine power has bestowed upon us all things that are requisite and suited to life and godliness, through the full personal knowledge of Him Who called us by and to His own glory excellence virtue.

V4- By means of these He has bestowed upon us His precious and exceedingly great promises, so that through them you may escape (by flight) from the moral decay that is in the world because of covetousness (lust and greed) , and become sharers (partakers) of the divine nature.

In verse 5, He starts to reason with us, and up to verse 9, shows the necessity, and goes on, " For whoever lacks... these qualities is blind, Spiritually short sighted, seeing only what is near to him, and has become oblivious to the fact that he was cleansed from his old sins.

V-10 " Because of this, brethren, be all the more silicious and eager to make sure to ratify, to strengthen, to make steadfast, your calling and election; for if you do this, you will never stumble or fall.

I like the parts that help my faith be strengthened, as we read the reminders of where we've come from, and how we used to think, before we were made alive, and where we are now. in Christlikeness with one another.

So then Christian, what type of purpose did God intend for you, what type of "Vessel" do you suppose He's directing you to be? This is the significance of a good church; They should be encouraging the growth and maturing of their flocks', offering classes of discipleship, ministry, evangelizing, my fav. "Bible doctrine". "That the man of God may be thoroughly equipped" able to do every good work, what is a "type" of work you are called to do?

> *Ephesians 2:10- " For we are God's own hand-iwork, (His workmanship), recreated in Christ Jesus, born anew that we may do those good works which God predestined and planned beforehand for us taking paths which He prepared ahead of time, that we should walk in them, living the good life which He prearranged and made ready for us to live.*

> *1 Corinthians 14:1- "* ***EAGERLY PURSUE*** *and seek to acquire this love, and earnestly desire and cultivate the spiritual endowments (gifts), especially that you may prophesy (interpret the divine will and purpose in inspired preaching and teaching).*

> *Ephesians 4:7- " Yet grace (God's unmerited favor) was given to each of us individually [not indiscriminately, but in different ways] in*

proportion to the measure of Christ's rich and bounteous gift.

Romans 12:3- " For by the grace of God given to me, I warn everyone among you not to estimate and think of himself more highly than he ought, but to rate his ability with sober judgment, each according to the degree of faith apportioned by God to him.

It would be a good idea for you to make a journal of notes and scripture reference for building what's known as an apologetic', like a book report that has to "flow", and not contradict itself, for instance, you wouldn't say that we get our wings when we die, why? There's no scripture reference, likewise we can't proclaim that "we" chose Christ into our life, why? Again, no Biblical reference, plus those who do proclaim that they chose Jesus into their life, "by their own free will", are merely victims of basics and easy believers' tactics that are "the broad path" (this is necessity for a Biblically functioning church); what is the narrow path ? *"Enter through the narrow gate; for wide is the gate and spacious and broad is the way that leads away to destruction, and many are those who are entering through it. Matthew 7:13*

So then, how does your church measure up' to doctrinal issues and purposes? What about discipleship? Do you fully understand that we were part of God's plan and written in the Book of Life'.

Before the foundation, God's foreknowledge of all things, echo's all thru scripture, and the same when Jesus shows up, as in all His dealings with all people, He knows our hearts! Look at John 10 closely. V26–29

> *"But you do not believe and trust and rely on Me because you do not belong to My fold [you are no sheep of Mine]. The sheep that are My own hear and are listening to My voice; and I know them, and they follow Me.*
>
> *And I give them eternal life, and they shall never lose it or perish throughout the ages.*
>
> *My Father, Who has given them to Me, is greater and mightier than all else.*

Is the concept of "a chosen people" from the beginning to the end of days; starting to form a sense of you belong' to the Kingdom? Based upon God's grace, not your works to become His "grafted in" to a chosen people, His elect, as we are known, for the main purpose of glorifying Jesus throughout all eternity. Let's consider John 17 -2-6-7-9-24

> *"That He may give eternal life to all whom You have given Him." I have manifested Your Name [I have revealed Your very Self], to the people whom You have given Me out of the*

world, they were Yours, and You gave them to Me, and they have obeyed and kept Your word.

"I am praying for them, I am not praying (requesting) for the world, but for those You have given Me, for they belong to You. All things that are Mine are Yours, and all things that are Yours belong to Me: And I am glorified in (through) them.

Father, I desire that they also whom You have entrusted to Me [as Your gift to Me] may be with Me where I am , so that they may see My glory, which You have given Me... Your love gift to Me: for You loved Me before the foundation of the world. We should always recognize from wince we came. The world. our new fishing hole'. our place for His ministry, and even our "growth happens " in our new providential areas of contact, then, in our new "born again" lives should bear witness of the fruits of His Children, and though we are in the world, we shouldn't be of this world and its so-called philosophies, let's consider a few passages on that matter, first John 14:17 " *The Spirit of Truth," Whom the world cannot receive (welcome, take to its heart), because it does not see Him or recognize* Him. But you know and recognize Him, for He lives with you constantly and will be in you.

2

WHY WOULD GOD CHOSE US?

"But when He, Who had chosen and set me apart, even before I was born and had called me by His grace {His unde-served favor and blessing}, saw fit and was pleased to reveal {unveil, disclose } His Son within me so that I might proclaim Him.. Galatians 1:15

We owe' our lives to God, we did nothing to receive this life, in the same way. Salvation is God's free gift, that brings a new spiritual birth, that is also God's doing, you did nothing, you were part of His eternal plan before the foundation of the world, and now that you have arrived, and the Spirit has called you; And you received the "gift" of salvation", something changes in all who are born of His Spirit, the understanding of "forgiveness" takes hold! Yes! the penalty for your sins has been removed by someone. {not you}. We can do nothing of ourselves to pre-pay our way into His glory, we can't buy salvation, or pray our way there as well, ...

John 1:13 says. We owe our spiritual birth to God, not by our will, not by our physical impulse, It's not as a result of our bloodline, {even Abraham's}, but we owe our birth to God!

Salvation is a free gift, we can't work our way into Glory, many Christians of this day, are deceived by pastors, Willfully contrary to Gods method of salvation, many think that their salvation was a result of a choice made by them, was it ..? Let's consider how many Bible verses support that theology. Zero! No wear. does the Bible proclaim that salvation is of man's will. Yet many are deceived into this heretical way of thinking! Now. on the other hand, the Bible has over 100 verses that proclaim that salvation is a free Gift of God.

> Ephesians 2:8-10` For it is by free grace {Gods unmerited favor} that you are saved {delivered from judgment and made partakers of Christ's salvation} through faith. And this salvation is not of yourselves {of your own doing,

Nowhere in Scripture does the Bible proclaim.

That "salvation " is accomplished by man's will! Instead, scripture declares salvation is by God's will.

Eph.2:8-10

It came not through your own striving, but it is the gift of God; not because works, lest any man or woman should boast. It is not the result of what anyone can possibly do, so no one can pride himself/herself in it or take glory to himself. For we are God's own handiwork {His workmanship}, rec-reated in Christ Jesus, {born anew} that we may do those good works which God predestined {planned beforehand} for us, taking paths which, He prepared ahead of time, that we should walk in them {living the good life which He prearranged and made ready for us to live}. Romans 9:16

So then, God's gift is not a question of human will and human effort ...but of God's mercy

1 Peter 2:8-10

And ,a Stone that will cause stumbling and a Rock that will give men offence; they stumble because they disobey and disbelieve God's Word, as those who reject Him were destined {appointed} to do.

But you are a chosen race, a royal priesthood, a dedicated nation, God's own purchased, special people, that you may set forth the wonderful deeds and display the virtues and perfections of Him Who called you out of darkness into His marvelous light.

> Once you were not a people at all, but now you are God's people; once you were unpitted, but now you are pitted and have received mercy.

James 2:5

> Listen my beloved brethren; Has not God chosen those who are poor in the eyes of the world to be rich in faith and in their position as believers and to inherit the kingdom which He has promised to those who love Him?

1 Corinthians 1:26-30

For simply consider your own calling, brethren, not many of you were considered to be wise according to human estimates and standards, not many influential and powerful, not many of high and noble birth,

No, for God selected {deliberately chose} what in the world is foolish to put the wise to shame, and what the world calls weak to put the strong to shame. And

God also selected {deliberately chose} what in the world is lowborn and insignificant and branded and treated with contempt, that He might depose and bring to nothing the things that are..

So that; no mortal man should have a pretense for glorying and boast in the presence of God.

But it is from Him that you have your life in Christ Jesus,

Whom God made our Wisdom from God,

And revealed to us a knowledge of the divine plan of salvation previously hidden, manifesting itself as our Righteousness thus making us upright and putting us in right standing with God.

Now, let's review Gods method of salvation, as Scripture proclaims, not what some pastor says, or even parents, we all must seek after what His Word is teaching us, in all of His plans, purposes', doctrines and decree's. Salvation is His freely given gift to us, in His timing, according to His design.

...none of which is done by us.

Now that we have received this wonderful gift.

We do have a responsibility to our Lord, the growth of our faith, sanctification participation, learning our ministry, proclaiming our testimonies, discovering His Wisdom, storing up knowledge, and So then, we must, believe His Word in "all" that it teaches" Obey "all" that it requires, and trust in all that it promises';

Now, Go teach all of it with Love.

The necessity of knowing this doctrine of election reveals to us a thankful ness for being chosen in the first place, and feel more loved, honored, humbled, secured in our walk with God, and qualified to go and share His Name.

Colossians 1:12-14

Giving thanks to the Father, who has qualified us and made us fit to share the portion which is the inheritance of the saints God's holy people in the light.

The Father has delivered and drawn us to Himself out of the control and dominion of darkness and has transferred us into the kingdom of the Son of His love.

Now then, the emphasis of our statements of faith, should be about.

"What has God called me to be"? Why would God choose me?

Instead of having a constant confusion about these matters, along with a sense of "you did this by your own free will" type mentality, and thus denying God the glory due to Him for giving us the gifts.

Let's consider Ephesians 2:8 & 9

> "For it is by free grace {God's unmerited favor} that you are saved, {delivered from judgment and made partakers of Christ's salvation} through faith. And this salvation is not of yourselves, {It is not of your own doing; it came not through your own striving} But it is the gift of God.

Not because of works, lest any man/ woman should boast, It is not the result of what anyone can possibly do, so no one can pride themselves in it or take glory to themself.

You see? We cannot, must not. say that we got our salvation as a result of our own will.

At this very moment, consider thanking God almighty for choosing you, and don't feel alone, even the apostles had a problem getting this!

Jesus himself describes to his disciples some' very to the point methods' of how the Spirit works, to whom it is given, and not.

> John 14:17 says, The Spirit of Truth, Whom the world cannot receive because it does not see Him or know and recognize Him,

but you know and recognize Him, for He
lives with you constantly and He will be
in you. John

15:16 You have not chosen Me, but I have
chosen you and have appointed you, that
you might go and bear fruit and keep on
bearing, that your fruit may be lasting, so
that whatever you ask the Father in My
Name, He may give it to you.

John 6:37 -65 `All whom My Father gives
to Me will come to Me".

V44~ "No one is able to come to Me unless the Father
Who sent Me attracts and draws him and gives him the
desire to come to Me.

V64 & 65~ But still some of you fail to believe and
trust and have faith. For Jesus knew from the first who did
not believe and had no faith and who would betray Him
and be false to Him. And He said,

this is why I told you that no one can come to Me
unless it is granted him by the Father.

So, by now you have a basic understanding of how the
method of salvation works; lets look in on Nicodemus, a
leader, an authority among the Jews. This man did not
understand, so he went to Jesus in the middle of the night,
to get this understanding...

So, Jesus explains to Nicodemus.

> John 3:6~"What is born of from the flesh is flesh, and what is born of the Spirit is Spirit, Marvel not at My telling you, you must all be born anew from above, The wind blows where it wills; and though you hear it's sound, yet you neither know where it comes from nor where it is going.

> So, it is with everyone who is born of the Spirit.

So then, have you received this "free" gift?

> John 1:12 &13~ But to as many as did receive and welcome Him, He gave the authority {power, privilege, right} to become the children of God, that is to those who believe in His Name. Who owe their birth neither to bloods nor to the will of the flesh {that of physical impulse}, nor to the will of man {that of a natural father}, but to God!

They are born of God !

3

COMMON MISTRANSLATIONS

John 3:16 is the most common misinterpret verse perhaps, let's peek.

For God so greatly loved the world, that He gave His only Son so that whoever {all the Gentiles; from all over the whole world} believes, trusts in, clings to, relies on .. Him, shall not perish! But have eternal life!

So yes, from every tribe, tongue, nation. these are known also by names, " the wild olive shoots", that were grafted in, As many as were "ordained" to eternal life and called by God.

So then, the verse means all men and women without distinction. let's consider the fact of the process of election as it is still intact, nothing changed, God still calls His Children.

> *Revelation 5:9- And now they sing a new song, saying, You are worthy to take the scroll and break the seals that are on it, for you were slain {sacrificed}, and with your blood* You purchased men unto God from every tribe and language and people and nation.

For many are called, but. not all, let's look at 1 Corinthians 1:26

> *For simply consider your own call, brethren; not many of you were considered to be wise according to human estimates and standards, not many influential and powerful, not many of high and noble birth. No for God selected {deliberately chose} what is in the world is called foolish to put to shame the wise, and what the world calls weak to put the strong to shame.*
>
> *V28- And God also chose {selected} what in the world is lowborn and insignificant and branded and treated with contempt, even the things that are nothing, that He might*

*depose and bring to nothing the things
that are. So that no mortal man should
boast in the presence of God.* You see? it is
done by God.

Similar to Ephesians 2:8 & 9- " And this salvation is
not of yourselves (of your own doing), it came not through
your own striving', but it is the gift of God; " Not because
of works ... Not the fulfillment of the Law's demands, lest
any man should, boast! You don't get to take credit for
salvation!

Remember. we must have a theology that flows. not
contradict.

Let's look at John 6:37-65- " All whom My Father gives
to Me will come to me: (these are the "elect".. past, present
& future.)

V44~ "No one is able to come to Me unless the Father
Who sent Me attracts and draws him, and gives him the
desire to come to Me, and then I will raise him up from
the dead at the last day.

*"All that the Father gives to Jesus", under-
standing this is crucial simply because, this
is the group of people that will have the...
Inheritance. The worldly ones do not; God
knows us all and did know us when He was
putting those who would receive His Word.
Consider John 14:17~ The Spirit of Truth',*

whom the world cannot receive because it does not see Him or know and recognize Him, but you know and recognize Him, for He lives with you constantly, and He will be in you. (The "world" will represent group "B".

Now then, we have group "A", those whom God "calls" ... and we have group "B", those who have been "condemned". Group "A" are written in the "Book of Life". unfortunately, those who would not receive Jesus, or His Word have a much different.

*Note: God knew all this before the foundation of the world.

Let's consider 1 Peter 2:7-10 " To you then who believe (who adhere to, trust in, and rely on Him) is the preciousness; but for those who disbelieve it is true; The very Stone which the builders rejected has become the main Cornerstone, also Psalms 118:22

And a Stone that will cause stumbling and a Rock that will give men offense; they stumble because they disobey and disbelieve God's Word, as those who reject Him were destined and appointed to do! ' So, take a breath and analyze yourself, do you believe it all? " *But you are a chosen race, a royal priesthood, a dedicated nation, God's Own Purchased Special People, that you may set forth the wonderful deeds and display the virtues and perfections of Him Who called you out of darkness into His Marvelous Light. Once you were not a people at all, but now you are God's people.*

So you see fellow" sinners and gentiles", we have been "given" a new life; that we did not deserve; So then sanctification begins. For the "child" of God is called out of darkness', and into His Marvelous Light, to keep himself from "worldly ways. Consider 2 Peter 1:1-10- V3~ " For His divine power has bestowed on us all things that are requisite and suited to life and godliness, through the full personal knowledge of Him Who called us by and to His Own glory and excellence. *(To become sharers of the divine nature, develop)*

Verses 5 through 8, explain to believer how they must grow, yes! We must do something! We must grow! Develop. WHY? Verse 9 says' ... For whoever lacks these qualities is blind! Spiritually shortsighted, seeing only what is near to him, and has become oblivious to the fact that he was cleansed from his old sins V10> Because of this, brethren, be all the more solicitous, and eager to make sure to (ratify, to strengthen, to make steadfast) you're calling and election; for if you do this, you will never stumble or fall.

Sanctification is the area in the believers walk that they develop into a "Christlike" being, in their forgiveness, and acts of Love. Here are but a few passages that further explain sanctification, one of my fav's. 2 Thessalonians 2:13 & 14- *"God chose you from the beginning as His first fruits, for salvation through the sanctifying work of the Holy Spirit and your belief in, and trust in the Truth. V14- It was to that end that He called you through our Gospel, so that you may obtain and share in the glory of our Lord Jesus Christ. " By now, you should be in understanding. " That freewill is not the method of salvation".*

1 Cor. 1:30 / 1 Thess. 4:3&4 / 2 Thess. 2:13-14 / 1 Peter 1:2 Conclusion; God calls us, If we receive His call, there is a Spiritual awakening to the facts of our sin, and the forgiveness from the penalties of our sins, and. what Jesus did through His death & resurrection, and how we develop and gain intrest in His Word.

How we approach God "reveals" much, even our identities, He just requires that we approach Him in Spirit & Truth' not nonsense, Let's consider Joh 4:23- A time will come, however, indeed it is already here, when the true worshipers will worship the Father in spirit and in truth (reality); for the Father is seeking just such people as these as His worshipers. V24> God is a Spirit (a spiritual Being) *and those who worship Him must worship Him in spirit and in truth. In the reality of what the Bible describes, Not conjecture!*

> *Remember. Salvation is not activated by our will, we really don't understand anything about God, until we are born again. As it is written, none is righteous, just, and truthful, no not one! No one understands (no one intelligently discerns or comprehends)*
>
> *No one seeks out God. ~ Romans 3:10f*

4

ADMONISH ONE
ANOTHER IN LOVE

* Finding unity, in Biblical concepts, doctrines, teachings.

The necessity of rebukes, reproofs, and admonishments are very necessary in the life and growth, of a Christian, none of us start out on this wonderful journey with a complete "roadmap" of how we get from our present location, to our new destination, nor what will happen along our way; so then, we should pay more attention to Biblical matters, because .."His Word matters", we should be good students of His Word, growing into spiritual knowledge & wisdom; This also shows our desires are clearly more focused, and will increase our ability to "get someone back on track". The trick? Getting people to listen! Consider *Psalm 81:8- "Hear, O My people, and I will admonish you! O Israel, if you would listen to Me"!* I recall *my first time that I was "helped" back on track, and also the first time that I admonished', and older widow lady, her belief of "our turning into angels"* after we pass away, was on her part very true, this seemed out of sorts to me so I asked her to understand that the Bible says something altogether different than her nice "belief" and thinking. However, was her thinking correct? No, it wasn't, just a visit to His Word was all that was required, plus, that first reproof also showed me something of what I was to become; (who I am now).

I try to imagine our patriarch Timothy, and the instruction he had to receive, and follow. 1 Timothy 5:20 says" As for those who are guilty and persist in sin, **rebuke and admonish them** in the presence of all. so that the rest may be warned and stand in.. Wholesome Awe and Fear

Let's define a term called *carnal Christianity,* {actually you look that one up} and knowing people by their "fruits".. Then, toss in the Matthew 7 passage "do not judge" one another, plus. esteem others better than yourself,

So then fellowship and stewardship are good goals of value and growth in the life of "hands on" training, on our way to being a SERVANT

Let's consider what kind of people will not inherit The Kingdom. 1 Corinthians 6:9- " Do you not know that the unrighteous and the wrongdoers will not inherit or have any share in the .... Kingdom of God?

Do not be deceived. Mislead; neither the impure and immoral, nor idolaters, ... nor adulteress, ... nor those who.... Participate in homosexuality.

We must also consider a couple things at this junction, first off; Let's look at verse 10- Nor cheats, nor greedy, nor drunkards, nor foulmouthed revilers and slanderers, nor extortioners and robbers, will inherit the kingdom of God, now then, consider yourself . How far in "darkness" were any of us? When God spoke to us, He revealed to us a few "awareness's" to our hearts *(spirits,) and* our sinfulness' and our Savior, Jesus Christ, that paid the penalty for that long list. When we " **receive "**our call from God, the born again' newness of life shows itself; virtually we see through a new viewing vantage point, never before seen by us, and we seek His Word, He reveals it to us, and we all have our own testimonies, we are all "called". Being "called" and "drawn" then, is our starting point, John 6:44 {Depending on our calling} 1 Corinthians 1:26ff

One of our goals then is to preserve the scripture, not pervert it. And that point leads to "the necessity for unity" in all that we believe, and in all that we obey. and in all that we hope to come.

We all have sinned and fall short of the requirements that we think we need to meet in order to be a follower of Christ; and we were all delivered out of the cesspool of the worlds muck and mires. Let's consider verse 11- And such some of you were once. But you were purified by a complete atonement for sin, and you were consecrated, and you were justified, (pronounced righteous), by trusting in the name of the Lord Jesus Christ and in the Holy Spirit. {Dependent upon Jesus} Romans 8: 28ff

Learning is essential, admonishment is needed for unity. So then one Christian (A) cannot say to Christian (B) that in order to pray, you must have a prayer "mat", what is wrong with that assertion? Very simple, it's not Biblical, it is a manmade concept. In the same way Bible doctrine (teachings) must be fact checked! When we find ourselves "mistaken" with concepts of the plans and purposes of God Almighty, we simply must "adjust" our thinking.

To His Instructions

Let's consider Romans 1:16-2:8. This is about those who deny God and the stubbornness of Homosexuals and the punishments that God imposes on them (V-16) For I am not ashamed of the Gospel (good news) of Christ, eternal death, to everyone who believes with a personal trust and a confident surrender and firm reliance, to the Jew first and also the Greek, (17) For in the Gospel a righteousness which God ascribes is revealed, both springing from faith leading to faith as it is written, The man who through faith is just and upright shall live and live by faith. (18) For God's Holy wrath and indignation are revealed from heaven against all ungodliness and unrighteousness of men, who in their wickedness repress and hinder the truth and make it inoperative. (19) For that which is known about God is evident to them and made plain in their inner consciousness, because God Himself has shown it to them. (20) For ever since the creation of the world His invisible nature and attributes, that is, His eternal power and divinity, have been made intelligible and clearly discernable in and through the things that have been made (His handiworks). So, men are without excuse altogether without any defense or justification. (21) Because when they knew and recognized Him as God, they did not honor and glorify Him as God or give Him thanks. But instead, they became futile and godless in their thinking with vain imaginings, foolish reasonings, and stupid speculations and their senseless minds were darkened (22) Claiming to be wise, they became fools professing to be smart, they made simpletons of themselves. (23) And by them the glory and majesty and excellence of the immortal God were exchanged for and represented by images, resembling mortal man, birds and beasts and reptiles. (24) Therefore God gave them up in the lusts of their own hearts to sexual impurity, to the dishonoring of their bodies among themselves, (abandoning them to the degrading power of sin). (25) Because they exchanged the truth of God for a lie and worshiped and served the creature rather than the Creator. Who is blessed forever! Amen. (26) For this reason, God gave them over and abandoned them to vile affections and degrading passions for their women exchanged their natural function for an unnatural and abnormal one. (27) And the men also turned from natural relations with women and were set ablaze burning with lust for one another- men committing shameful acts with men .. and suffering their own bodies and personalities. the inevitable consequences and penalty of their wrongdoing and going astray, which was their fitting retribution. (28) And so, since they did not see fit to acknowledge God or approve of Him or consider Him worth the knowing, God gave them over to a base and condemned mind to do things not proper or decent *but* loathsome. (29) Until they were filled (saturated) with every kind of unrighteousness, iniquity, grasping and covetous greed, and malice, They were full of envy and jealousy, murder, strife, deceit and treachery, ill will and cruel ways, they are secret backbiters and gossipers, slanders, hateful to and hating God, full of insolence, arrogance, and boasting; inventors of new forms of evil; disobedient and unfruitful to parents. (31) They were without understanding, conscienceless and faithless, heartless and loveless and merciless. (32) Though they are fully aware of God's righteous decree that those who do such things deserve to die, they not only do them themselves but approve and applaud others who practice them.

Chapter 2 Therefore You have no excuse or defense or justification.

So then, is this hate speech? Some would say yes, well, this is God's decree, His outlook upon such individuals, not mine, I am only the messenger, we are called to give God's Gospel message to everyone. gays included, however, the light of repentance needs to work hand in hand with confession in a prayerful mindset, a pastor must speak to the reality of a sinner's destiny, as with us all in mind, as we console one another, this confession one-to-another'. must surely take place; it is difficult to explain to a gay person that they are in sin, sometimes that fails at first, many pastors fail miserably at giving Biblical scripture, and so then, just pat the sinner on the back and affirm them in their sin, and some think homosexuality is just normal for a believer. So, pastors must set the sacred boundaries for their flocks, tending to their flocks, maybe even put up' no trespassing signs' in their sermons in a loving and caring manner. In Spirit and in Truth.

> *Let's consider Colossians 3:16~ Let the Word spoken by Christ the Messiah have its home in your hearts and minds and dwell in one another in all insight and intelligence and wisdom in spiritual things, and as you sing psalms and hymns and spiritual songs, making melody to God with His grace in your hearts.*

5

Do Not Be Deceived

We must approach the working out of our salvation, knowing where we need growth, more understanding, taking steps to grow and fine tune the gifts that God has blessed each one with.

Step one, approach God in "Spirit and Truth".

Step two, Analyze Our sinfulness, & His Sacrifice.

Step three, learning to stay in alignment with Him.

We have an increased awareness of our fallen conditions, we also develop new standards as new vantage points open up, and new dimensions of complications also increase, *just sayin'*

Our new life becomes more in every way, more complex, more complicated, fuller in Christ, when we engage ourselves.

Having engaged ourselves, we soon discover that many professing Christians, don't agree with one another very well, they insist on having some *"man-made"* tradition that Biblically doesn't exist. This particular "gray" area is the cause for the most **Deception.**

Fact checking *what* **is being preached (anywhere), creates a problem with some clergy, when presenting them with Biblical scripture that doesn't support their particular convoluted ideas. All through time, smooth talking pastors, clergy, etc. have led God's children down the wrong path, this is perhaps the area that presents the greatest challenge for growing Christians; So then... Brace up and reinvigorate and set right your slackened and weakened and drooping hands and strengthen your feeble and palsied and tottering knees and cut through and make firm and plain and smooth, strait paths for your feet [yes make them safe and upright and happy paths that go in the right direction], so that the lame may not be put out of joint, but rather may be cured.**

In order not to be deceived, we come to see the evil one as our greatest source of lies and temptations, however, we live in a fallen world, fires, floods, earth quakes, and so forth, is another type of force that we have to bear, on our lands, in our homes, all can be wiped away, a volcano can just make it disappear, so the fallen world is always there for us to experience and deal with.

The fallenness of mankind' is the next thing to be aware of in our spiritual growth, first part is our fleshly

desires, and learning "self-control" in those areas that we sometimes struggle in . next up .. the rest of the living population around us, all those not written in The Book of Life, you know them, we all are sewn in together, and grow together, it also is clear that we must witness to the lost, *It is from that quagmire of darkness that we all come,* Then, from that spiritually blind and dead condition, You He made alive, are you not aware of that ? *Ephesians 1 & 2*

> " *Do you not know that the unrighteous and the wrongdoers will not inherit or have any share in the kingdom of God?*
>
> " *Do not be Deceived. or misled; neither the impure and immoral, nor idolaters, nor adulterers, nor those who participate in homosexuality. 1 Corinthians 6:9*
>
> " **Holding fast to faith (that leaning of the entire human personality of God in absolute trust and confidence) and having a good clear conscience. By rejecting and thrusting from them, some individuals have made shipwreck of their faith.** 1 Timothy 1:19

"But the Holy Spirit distinctly and expressly declares that in the latter times some will turn away from the faith. giving attention to deluding and seducing spirits and doctrines that demons teach". 1 Timothy 4:1

" Guard and keep with the greatest care the precious and excellently adapted Truth which has been entrusted to you by the help of the Holy Spirit Who makes His home in us." 2 Tim. 1:14

" Do not be deceived and deluded and misled; God will not allow Himself to be sneered at or mocked; For whatever a man sows, that is only what he will reap". Galatians 6:7

" For we also were once thoughtless and senseless, obstinate and disobedient, deceived, deluded, misled; we too were once slaves to all sorts of cravings and pleasures, wasting our days in malice and jealousy and envy, hateful and hating one another." Titus 3:3

" Do not be deceived or misled; neither the impure and immoral, nor idolaters, nor

adulterers, nor those who participate in homosexuality, will not have any share in the Kingdom of God." 1 Corinthians 6:9

" *But wicked men and imposters will go from bad to worse, deceiving and leading astray others and being deceived and led astray themselves.* 2 Timothy 3:13

" *For you yourselves know perfectly well that the day of the return of the Lord will come as unexpectedly and suddenly as a thief in the night".* 1 Thessalonians 5:2

" *But you are not in darkness, brethren, for that day to overtake you by surprise like a thief."* 1 Thessalonians 5:4

" *The Spirit of Truth, Whom the world cannot receive, because it does not see Him or know and recognize Him, but you know and recognize Him, for He lives with you constantly and will be in you ".* John 14:17

We started in this chapter with scripture that declares our duty to not be deceived in various areas, and there's an abundance of more such verses that warn the believers to not be deceived, that includes all of us born again Christians, most warnings are about the second coming of Christ, review Matthew 24:23-26-42

> *" See, I have warned you beforehand.*

> *" Watch therefore {give strict attention, be cautious and active}*

> *" Let no one deceive or beguile you in any way, for that day will not come except the apostasy comes first (unless the predicted great falling away of those who professed to be Christians has come) and the man of lawlessness (sin) is revealed, who is the son of... doom, (of perdition).* 2 Thessalonians 2:3

So then, we must certainly look into these areas so that we may not be deceived in any way, by anyone, simply because we must believe His Word of Truth, in all that it says, if not , we'll find ourselves being led astray, you see, If you don't stand for His Truth, you'll fall for anything, and then we really go down the slippery slope of mis-truths, half-truths, all of which are short of His Word.

> *"Therefore, God sends upon them a misleading influence, a working of error and*

a strong delusion to make them believe what is false, in order that all may be judged and condemned who did not believe in the Truth, instead took pleasure in unrighteousness."

2 Thessalonians 2:11&12

6

OUR PARTS IN SANCTIFICATION

We must understand that the father has drawn us to himself out of the control of the dominion of darkness and has transferred us into the Kingdom of the son of his love in whom we have our redemption through his blood, so we as numerous as we are in one body in Christ and as individuals we are part of one another having gifts that are different according to the grace given us, so then our purposes have to be aligned with gods purposes.

Ephesians 2 verse 10 says for we are God's own handiwork his workmanship recreated in Christ born and knew that we may do those good works which God predestined planned beforehand for us that we should take paths which he prepared ahead of time and that we should walk in them living the good life which he prearranged and made ready for us to live in. It's hard for us to think outside of time however, we must understand if we are to fully appreciate the many ways in which we are all blessed and how we become even further blast as we give ourselves to one another.

God has a purpose for each one of us, so along with finding our God-given identity we also must look at our purpose that he gave us. Sanctification is the growth in our spiritual maturity and it continues until we leave this planet, so then It's how we measure our walk in Christ, God will give us opportunities to hone our skills that he has set apart for us, he wants to make us complete and usable for every good work, so having a good focus on our relationship with Christ in our everyday comings and goings, and we will start to see the times when we fall short as his adopted children, and we will soon understand we do not want to fall short of anything that God has shown to us.

We are being made ready to reap and sow eternal things so we should naturally let go of worldly things or temporal things, that is part of the change we have gone through in our rebirth, it is just hard to remember to always follow.

One way to look at our sanctification is to consider our spiritual maturity and transformation Let's consider second Peter, chapter one verse 3 says for his divine power has bestowed upon us all things that are requisite and suited to life and godliness through the full personal knowledge of him who called us by and to his own glory an excellent virtue. Verse 4 by means of these he has bestowed upon us his precious and exceedingly great promises so that through them you may escape from the moral decay the rottenness and corruption that is in the world because of covetousness lust and greed, and become sharers and partakers of the divine nature, verse 5 for this very reason adding your diligence to the divine promises, employ every effort in exercising your faith to develop virtue, and in exercising virtue develop knowledge and intelligence, verse 6 and an exercise thing knowledge develop self-control, and in exercising self-control develop steadfastness and patience and endurance, and in exercising godliness develop brotherly affection, and in exercising brotherly affection develop Christian love.

Verse 8 four as these qualities are yours and increasingly abound in you, they will keep you from being idle or unfruitful unto the full personal knowledge of our Lord Jesus Christ the Messiah. Verse 9 for whoever lacks these qualities is blind spiritually short sighted seeing only what is near to him and has become oblivious to the fact that he was cleansed from his old sins. Verse 10 pay close attention to this verse because of these brethren be all the more salacious and eager to make sure to ratify to strengthen and to make steadfast your calling and election, for if you do these things you will never stumble or fall verse 11 thus there will be richly and abundantly provided for, and your entry into the eternal Kingdom of our Lord and savior Jesus Christ. I like to reflect on this, and so should you have you made sure you have ratified you're calling and election? This is the area in which we must engage ourselves and Stand firm in our faith and turning away from worldly desires. have you really escaped from the moral decay the rottenness and corruption that is in the world? this is something we must do in our everyday walk. It's kind of like the light that illuminates our path as we gather Nuggets of God's truth along the way we build our theology ,the further we seek, the brighter the light becomes, that's why correction is so important, because it leads all the spirit filled believers to the unity of the truth, and truth is the only way to honestly and reverently approach God, many times in scripture it tells us God can only be approached in Spirit and in Truth that's how He has set this up: in our relationship with Him and those around us that are seeking the Truth, Second Timothy 3: 16 Says for every scripture is God breathed given by his inspiration, and profitable for instruction, for reproof and conviction of sin, for correction of error and discipline in obedience, and for training and righteousness in holy living, in conformity to God's will in thought, purpose, and action, so that the man of God may be complete and proficient well fitted and thoroughly equipped for every good work.

OK let's go back to second Peter chapter one verse 19

And we have the prophetic word made firmer still, you would do well to pay close attention to it as to a lamp shining in a dismal squalid and dark place, until the day breaks through the gloom and then the morning star rises, and it comes into your being in your hearts.

You see God has clothed the dust in new clothing, You don't even want to wear the clothes you wore before you became spiritually aware of who you are now and where you're going now, and it is a great privilege to be called by God, and it deserves our full attention and devotion, and yes, our responsibilities of this relationship are a privilege now with the greater privilege, Also comes the greater responsibilities, for instance the greeter is doing something at the door, but the choir is involved in something a little more complex, also the pastor is involved in yet something even more complex, they're all part of the same worship event, yet each has a different role to play out according to what he has been given.

The understandings and our purposes given to us in Christ are sometimes hard to conceive, for instance you may be the greeter you volunteered for that position, and you have been doing the greeting at your church for over a year now, but people have been hearing you singing while you've been greeting, and they think that you should try out for the choir, so you try out for the choir and now you are part of a much larger picture, and now you learn how to read the music, and you're singing improves, and you pick up the guitar and learn to play it well, now you have done this for over a year, and they want you to become worship director, and so you pursue with vigor and a desire to worship the Lord in a much bigger way now than you ever have before, then one day while you were leading the praise team in your prayer, they noticed how deeply and sincerely you pray and how all-inclusive you are in your prayers to the almighty.

Then one day the pastor of your church has died, there is no one now at your church to lead the congregation, but those who have been around you that have heard you praying, and that has seen your growth in the Lord suggest that you be the pastor of the church at least until a new pastor with credentials arrives.

And you accept this position that God has called you too, and He has trained you up in and for this position, yeah it's there you go fish, now, you look back when you were the praise and worship leader, you probably never would have imagined that you would be the pastor of this church at some point, and while you were the greeter you probably never thought that you would be a part of the choir, but now we start to see that with God all things are possible, we must apply ourselves to the callings as they come to us, it is God who calls us to do these things, it's up to us to receive them all.

The process of spiritual transformation is known as our sanctification, it is the process of that growth in this life, that prepares us for the next. God has set us apart from the world spiritually, but physically in this fleshly body, that we temporarily habitat in, we will sometimes find it more difficult and even opposition and challenge in our everyday lives.

Many times in scripture God shows that He not only tests us but He chastens us because we are His children

,so based on that alone we should understand a few things that come into our lives, next we have to consider that the devil, wants to ruin us and our relationship with Christ by his lies and accusations, it is up to us to keep that light of love and truth alive in our hearts, and if we are diligently seeking God and how we stand before him in our relationship we will always seek to improve that's how the method of sanctification is meant to work and that's how the Spirit takes us through each and every step of this learning process of letting go of our worldly passions, yet hanging on to what is good and given by God.

So having a good sense of biblical awareness of God's purposes plans and his laws, is essential for all Christians, we are supposed to be about collecting His knowledge and understanding in order that we may not perish in our ignorance. We should be applying this knowledge that we have collected in our ministry in our words in our hearts and in our goals of edifying the Saints to unity of his truth that he has given us, all of us.

The illumination of our walk started when we received God's spirit into our hearts when He came knocking at our door when He called us out of darkness and into His marvelous light, we freely came and it was beautiful and we see that we were forgiven in our sins, and we start to get a picture of what Jesus did at the cross and as your little light gets more and more illuminated in sincerity and humility we come to knowledge how God sees us and how He wants us to change these sinful positions that we hold and partake in, so in this case God will remind us in His chastisements of us by the events of life that go on around us if He can't get our attention by His Word, He will get our attention by some other means, but change is always required in each of us, we are constantly reminded in scripture that we are to grow were to stop drinking the basic milk of scripture at some point and start to digest the harder things of His plans and purposes for each of us, and that takes a lifetime.

Learning to receive God's gifts always takes us in a new direction and causes us to speak the word, it causes us to share our testimony, it leads us to spiritual maturity, and leads us to worship with others and glorify him with our hearts and our voices because we're ever growing into and finding our ultimate purpose in the Kingdom with an outward display of our inward illuminated spirits and our trueness of our hearts in the word with others and this gospel will arouse his children. Because whatever we are growing into, He knew, already.

7

SEVEN STEPS

#1 This is a Review list of scripture that declares our salvation is His gift to us, we are drawn or called to Himself, when we receive our calling, it first calls us to repentance, and also to Jesus as the atonement (payment) for our sins we've collected along the way, however', one cannot stay in position of just "believing", that is a fruitless relationship at-best. we must seek out God's plans & purposes. as we seek, we find, so then the truth of scripture builds itself in us as we collect more and more. Built upon the "Cornerstone", the nuggets of truth that we collect about all His doctrines, plans, and purposes, and the providential opportunities, that He has planned for us, even the things that we think are coincidental, are really done by His hand, we should come to expect Him. remember... We are part of a "Royal Priesthood", and we must stand in His "Truth", Armor up'~ Ephesians 6, In Spirit and Truth.

He chose you, and foreknew you, and did write you in His "Book of Life"

Note*- There is no place in scripture that says" we chose God.

We will start in the New Testament, mainly because many Christians believe Election and Gods chosen are a "Old Testament" doctrine, Old Testament scriptures will follow in our review.

> *Matthew 5:10- "Blessed and happy and enviably fortunate and spiritually pros-perous in the state in which the born-again child of God enjoys and finds satisfaction in God's favor and salvation."*

> *Matthew 12:18- " Behold My Servant Whom I have chosen, & I will put My Spirit upon him."*

> *Matthew 20:16- 22:14-" For many are called, but few chosen."*

> *Matthew 24:31- " And He will send out His Angels with a loud trumpet call, and they will gather His elect (His Chosen Ones)*

from the four winds, [even] from one end of the universe to the other.

Luke 10:20- " Nevertheless, do not rejoice at this, that the spirits are subject to you, but rejoice that your names are enrolled in heaven."

Luke 18:7- " And will not our just God defend and protect and avenge His elect (His chosen ones), who cry out to Him night and day ? Will He defer them and delay help on their behalf?

Luke 24:45- " Then He thoroughly opened up their minds to understand the scriptures".

*John 1:12&13- " But to as many as did receive and welcome Him, He gave the power, the privilege, the right to become the children of God, that is, to those who believe in, adhere to, trust in, and rely on His Name, who owe their birth. Neither to bloods nor to the will of the flesh [**that of physical impulse]** nor to the will of man [**that of a natural father]**, ..But to God*

John 3:8- " The wind blows where it wills; and though you hear its sound, yet you neither know where it comes from nor where it is going. So, it is with everyone who is born of the Spirit.'

John 4:23-24- " A time will come, however, indeed it is already here, when the true (genuine) worshipers will worship the Father in spirit and in truth; for the Father is seeking just such people as these as His worshipers. God is a Spirit (a spiritual Being) and those who worship Him in Spirit and in Truth.

John 6:37- " All whom My Father gives Me will come to Me.

John 6:44 -" No one can come to Me unless the Father Who sent Me attracts and draws him and gives him the desire to come to Me, and then I will raise him up from the dead at the last day.

John 6:63-65-" It is the Spirit Who gives life {He is the life- giver} the flesh conveys no benefit whatever (there is no profit in it). The Words (Truths) that I have been speaking to you are ...

Spirit and life

" *But still, some of you fail to believe and trust and have faith. For Jesus knew from the first who did not believe and had no faith and who would betray Him and be false to Him.*

"And He said, this is why I told you that no one can come to Me unless it is granted him [unless he is enabled to do so] by the **Father.**
* Method of salvation note: *John 6:63-65*

John 10:26-29- " *But you do not believe and trust and rely on Me because you do not belong to My fold [you are no sheep of Mine]. The sheep that are My own hear and are listening to My voice: and I know them, and they follow Me. And I give them eternal life, and they shall never lose it or perish throughout the ages. And no one can snatch them out of My Fathers hand.*

" *My Father, who has given them to Me, is greater and mightier than all else; and no one is able to snatch them out of the ...*

Fathers Hand.

John 13:17-20- "If you know these things, blessed and happy and to be envied are you if you practice them, I am not speaking of and do not mean all of you. **I know whom I have chosen;** *but that the scripture may be fulfilled, He who eats My bread with Me has raised up his heel against Me. I assure you, most solemnly I tell you, he who receives and welcomes and takes into his heart any messenger of Mine receives Me [in just that way]; and he who receives and welcomes and takes Me into his heart receives Him Who sent Me [in the same way].*

John 14:17-" The Spirit of Truth, Whom the world cannot receive (welcome, take to its heart), because it does not see Him or know and recognize Him. But you know and rec- ognize Him, for He lives with you constantly and will be in you.

John 15:16 & 19b- " You have not chosen Me, " but I have chosen you and have appointed you {I have planted you }, that you might go and bear fruit and keep bearing;- " But I have chosen [selected] you out of the world, the world hates you.

John 17:6-9-" I have manifested Your Name to the people whom You have given Me out of the world. They were Yours, and You gave them to Me, and they have obeyed and kept Your Word.

" I am praying for them, I am not praying for the world, but for those You have given Me, for they belong to You.

Acts 2:39- " For the promise of the Holy Spirit is to and for you and your children, and to and for all that are far away, even to and for as many as the Lord our God invites and bids to come to Himself.

Acts 10:41- " Not by all the people but to us who were chosen (designated) beforehand by God as witnesses, who ate and drank with Him after He arose from the dead.

Acts 10:41- " And the believers from among the circumcised who came with Peter were surprised and amazed, because the free gift of the Holy Spirit had been bestowed and poured out largely even on the Gentiles.

Acts 13:48-" And when the Gentiles heard this, they rejoiced and glorified (praised and gave thanks for) the Word of God; and as many as were destined [appointed and ordained] to eternal life believed [adhered to, trusted in, and relied on Jesus as the Christ and their savior "].

Acts 22:14-" And he said, " The God of our forefathers has destined and appointed you to come progressively to know His will [to perceive, to recognize more strongly and clearly, and to become better and more intimately acquainted with His will, and to see the Righteous One and to hear a voice from His own mouth and a message from His own lips.

Romans 4:16- " Therefore, inheriting the promise is the outcome of faith and depends entirely on faith, in order that it might be given as an act of grace.

Romans 5:2- " Through Him also we have our access [entrance, introduction] by faith into this grace [state of God's favor] in which we firmly and safely stand. And let us rejoice and exult in our hope of experiencing and enjoying the glory of God".

Romans 8:15- " For the Spirit which you have now received is not a spirit of slavery to put you once more in bondage to fear, but you have received the Spirit of adoption, the Spirit producing sonship in the bliss of which we cry, Abba Father!

Romans 8:28- 30 " We are assured and know that God being a partner in their labor all things work together and are fitting into a plan for good to and for those who love God and are called according to His design and purpose. For those whom He foreknew [of whom He was aware of and loved beforehand] , **He also destined from the beginning [foreordaining them]** *to be molded into the image of His Son, and share inwardly His likeness, that He might become the firstborn among many brethren, and those whom* **He thus foreordained, He also called, He also justified, acquitted, made righteous. and those whom He**

justified. He also glorified *raising them to a heavenly dignity and condition.*

Romans 8:33-" Who shall bring any charge against God's elect?

Romans 9:11- " And the children were yet unborn and had so far done nothing either good or evil. Even so, in order further to carry out God's purpose of selection (election), which depends not on works or what men can do, but on Him Who calls them.

Romans 9:16- " So then, God's gift is not a question of human will and human effort, but of God's mercy, [it depends not on one's own willingness, nor on his strenuous exertion as in running a race, but on God's having mercy on him.

Romans 9:32- " For what reason? Because they pursue it not through faith, relying instead on the merit of their works, they did not depend on faith but on what they could do. They have stumbled over the Stumbling Stone."

Romans 11:2- " No, God has not rejected and disowned His people whose destiny He had marked out and appointed and fore-known from the beginning. Do you not know what the scripture says" ...?

Romans 11:5- " So too at the present time there is a remnant, selected (chosen) by grace (God's unmerited favor and graciousness).

Romans 11:7- " What then shall we con-clude? Israel failed to obtain what it sought [God's favor by obedience to the Law]. Only the elect (those chosen few) obtained it, while the rest of them became callously indifferent, (they were blinded, hardened, and made insensible to it.") V8-" As it is written, God gave them a spirit (an atti-tude) of stupor, eyes that should not see and ears that should not hear, that has con-tinued down to this very day.

Romans 11:28- " But from the point of view of God's choice (of election), of divine selec-tion, they (the Jews) are still the beloved [dear to Him] for the sake of their forefa-thers, For God's gifts and His callings are irrevocable, (He never withdraws them when once they are given, and does not change His mind about those to whom He gives His grace or to He sends His call).

1 Corinthians 1:2b-" To those consecrated and purified and made holy in Christ Jesus, who are selected and called to be saints [God's people], together with all those who in any place call upon and give honor to the Name of our Lord Jesus Christ, both their Lord and ours, v9- by Him you were called into companionship and participation with His Son, Jesus Christ our Lord. v24- To the Gentiles it is absurd and utterly unphilosophical nonsense... "But to those who are called, whether Jew or Greek (Gentile), Christ is the power of God and the Wisdom of God.

1 Corinthians 1:26-" For simply consider your own call, brethren; not many of you were considered to be wise according to human standards and estimates, not many influential and powerful, not many of high and noble birth. V27-" No for God selected [deliberately chose] what is foolish to put the wise to shame, and what the world calls weak to put the strong to shame. V28-" And

God also selected [deliberately chose] what in the world is lowborn and insignificant and branded and treated with contempt, even the things that are nothing, that He might depose and bring to nothing the things that are. So that no moral man should have pretense for glorying and boast in the presence of God V30-" But it from Him that you have your life in Christ Jesus, Whom God made our Wisdom from God, revealed to us a knowledge of the divine plan of salvation previously hidden, manifesting itself as our Righteousness thus making us upright and putting us in right standing with God, and our Consecration making us pure and holy, and our Redemption, providing our ransom from eternal penalty for sin.

1 Corinthians 2:12-" Now we have not received the spirit that belongs to the world, but the Holy Spirit Who is from God, given to us that we might realize and comprehend and appreciate the gifts of divine favor and blessing so freely and lavishly and bestowed on us by God. And we are setting these truths forth in words not taught by human wisdom but taught by the Holy Spirit, combining, and

intercepting spiritual truths with spiritual language to those who possess the Holy Spirit.

2 Corinthians 1:12-" It is a reason for pride and exultation to which our conscience testifies that we have conducted ourselves in the world especially towards you, with devout and pure motives and Godly sincerity, not in fleshly wisdom but by the grace of God, which God, exerting His holy influence upon souls, turns them to Christ, and keeps them and strengthens and increases them in Christian virtues. V21-" But it is God Who confirms and makes us steadfast and establishes us in joint fellowship with you in Christ, and has consecrated and anointed us, enduing us with the gifts

.... of The Holy Spirit.

2 Corinthians 6:1-" Laboring together' as God's fellow workers with Him then, we beg of you not receive the grace of God in vain [that merciful kindness by which God exerts His Holy influence on souls and turns them to Christ keeping and strengthening them]– Do not receive it to no purpose, for He says,

*in the time of favor (of an assured welcome),
I have listened to and heeded your call, and
I have helped you on the day of deliverance
(the day of salvation). Behold, now is truly
the time for a gracious welcome and accep-
tance of you from God, behold now is the
day of salvation.*

*Galatians 1:15-" But when He, who had
chosen and set me apart even before I was
born and had called me by His grace, His
undeserved favor and blessing, saw fit and
was pleased.*

*Galatians 3:26-" For in Christ Jesus you are
all sons of God through faith, for as many of
you as were baptized into Christ into a spiritual union and communion with Christ.
the Anointed One.*

*Galatians 5:7-" You were running the race
nobly, who has interfered (stopped you) hin-
dered you from following the Truth? This
evil persuasion is not from Him Who called
you, who invited you to freedom in Christ.*

*Ephesians 1:4-" Even as in His love He chose
us (actually picked us out for Himself as His*

own), in Christ before the foundation of the world, that we should be holy, consecrated and set apart for Him, and blameless in His sight, even above reproach, before Him in love, V5- "For He foreordained us, destined us, planned in love for us to be adopted and revealed as His own children through Jesus Christ, in accordance with the purpose of His will, because it pleased Him and was His kind intent.

Ephesians 1:11-" In Him we also were made God's heritage (portion) and we obtained an inheritance; for we had been foreordained, chosen and appointed beforehand in accordance with His purpose, who works out everything in agreement with the counsel and design of His own will. V13-" In Him you also, who have heard the Word of Truth, the glad tidings (Gospel) of your salvation, and have believed in and adhered to and relied on Him. And you were stamped with the seal of the long-promised Holy Spirit.

Ephesians 2CC-" For you He made alive when you were dead and slain by your trespasses, V3- We were then by nature children in His of God's wrath and heirs of His indignation, like the rest of mankind, but God—- so rich is He in His mercy! Because of and in order to satisfy the great and wonderful and intense love with which Ho loved us V5- Even when we were dead (slain) by our own shortcomings and trespasses, He made us alive together in fellowship and union with Christ; (He gave us the very life of Christ Himself, the same new life with which He quickened Him), for it is by grace (His favor and mercy which you did not deserve), that you are saved, [delivered from judgement], and made partakers of Christ's salvation.

V8-" For it by free grace (God's unmerited favor) that you are saved (delivered from judgment) and made partakers of Christ's salvation, through faith, and this salvation is not of yourselves [of your own doing] it came not through your own striving....but

.. " It is the gift of God ".

V9-" Not because of works [not the fulfillment of the Law's demands], lest any man should boast, [it is not the result of what *anyone can possibly do], so no one can pride himself in it or take **glory to himself.***

V10-" For we are God's own handiwork (His workmanship), recreated in Christ Jesus, born anew, that we may do those good works which God predestined [planned beforehand] for us taking paths which He prepared ahead of time, that we should walk in them, [living the good life which He prearranged and made ready for us to live.

4:7-" Yet grace (God's unmerited favor) was given to each of us individually, not indiscriminately, but in different ways, in proportion to the measure of Christ's rich and bounteous gift.

6:19-" And pray also for me, that freedom of utterance may be given me, that I may open my mouth to proclaim boldly the mystery of the good news (the Gospel).

Colossians 1:12-" Giving thanks to the Father, Who has qualified and made us fit to share the portion which is the inheritance of the saints (God's chosen holy people) in the light. The Father has delivered and drawn us to Himself out of the control and the dominion of darkness and has transferred us into the kingdom of the Son of His love.

1 Thessalonians 1:4-" O brethren beloved by God, we recognize and know that He has selected (chosen) you. 5:24- " Faithful is He Who is calling you to Himself, and utterly trustworthy, and He will also do it [fulfill His call by hallowing and keeping you].

2 Thessalonians 2:13-" But we brethren beloved by the Lord, ought to and are obligated [as those who are in debt] to give thanks always to God for you, because God chose you from the beginning as His first fruits (first converts) for salvation through the sanctifying work of the Holy Spirit and your belief in adherence to trust in, and reliance on the Truth.

2 Timothy 1:9-" (For it is He) Who delivered and saved us and called us with a calling in itself holy and leading to holiness, to a life of consecration a vocation of holiness, He did it not because of anything of merit that we have done, but because of and to further His own purpose and grace [unmerited favor] which was given us in Christ Jesus before the world began. [eternal ages ago].

2 Timothy 2:10-" Therefore I am ready to persevere and stand my ground with patience and endure everything for the sake of the elect, God's chosen; so that they too may obtain the salvation, which is in Christ Jesus, with the reward of eternal glory.

Titus 1:1- " Paul, A bond servant of God and apostle (a special messenger) of Jesus Christ (the Messiah), to stimulate and promote the faith of God's chosen ones and to lead them on to accurate discernment and recognition of and acquaintance with the Truth which belongs to and harmonizes with and tends to godliness.

Titus 2:14-" Who gave Himself on our behalf that He might redeem us (purchase our freedom) from all iniquity and purify for Himself a people [to be peculiarly His own, people who are] eager and enthusiastic about living a live that is good and filled beneficial deeds.

Titus 3:7-" (And He is in order) that we might be justified by His grace, by His favor, wholly undeserved, that we might be acknowledged and counted as conformed to the divine will in purpose, thought, and action, that we might become heirs of eternal life according to our hope.

Hebrews 2:13-" And again He says, My Trust and assured reliance and confident hope shall be fixed in Him. And yet again, Here I am, I and the children whom God has given Me.

Hebrews 5:9- " And making Him perfectly equipped, He became the Author and Source of eternal salvation to all those who give heed and obey Him.

Hebrews 6:10-" For God is not unrighteous to forget or overlook your labor and the love which you have shown for His Name's sake in ministering to the needs of the saints [His own consecrated people], as you still do.

Hebrews 9:15-" Christ the Messiah is therefore the Negotiator and Mediator of an entirely New Testament (covenant) so that those who are called and offered it, may receive the fulfillment of the promised everlasting inheritance.

James 2:5-" Listen, my beloved brethren; Has not God chosen those who are poor in the eyes of the world, to be rich in faith and in their position as believers to inherit the kingdom which He promised to those who love Him?

James 4:5- Or do you suppose that the Scripture is speaking to no purpose that says, The Spirit Whom He has caused to dwell in us, yearns over us and He yearns for the Spirit to be welcome with a jealous love?

1 Peter 1f the elect exiles, who were chosen and foreknown by God the Father and consecrated, sanctified, made holy by the Spirit, to be obedient to Jesus Christ (the Messiah).

1 Peter 2:7-10-" To you then who believe (who adhere to, trust in , and rely on Him) is the preciousness; but those who disbelieve it is true, The very Stone which the builders rejected has become the main Cornerstone, and A Stone that will cause stumbling and a Rock that will give men offense; they stumble because they disobey and disbelieve God's Word, as those who reject Him were destined (appointed) to do.

"But you are a chosen race", a royal priesthood, a dedicated nation, God's own purchased, special people, that you may set forth the wonderful deeds and display the virtues and perfection of Him Who called you out of darkness into His marvelous light.

1 Peter 3:9 Loving others, and know that to this you have been called, that you yourselves inherit a blessing from God- that you may obtain a blessing as heirs.

1 Peter 5:10- " And after you have suffered a little while, the God of all grace, Who imparts all blessing and favor, Who has called you to His own eternal glory in Christ Jesus, will Himself complete and make you what you ought to be, established and ground you securely, and strengthen, and settle you.

2 Peter 1:3-10-" For His divine power has bestowed upon us all things that are requisite

67

and suited to life and godliness, through the full personal knowledge of Him Who called us by and to His own glory and excellence, by means of these He has bestowed upon us His great promises, so that through them you may escape the moral decay that is in the world, because of lust and greed, and have become partakers of the divine nature.

"For this very reason, adding to your diligence to the divine promises, employ every effort in exercising your faith to develop virtue, excellence and resolution, and in exercising virtue, develop knowledge, (Intelligence). For as these qualities are yours and increasingly abound in you, -V9- " For whoever lacks these qualities is blind, (spiritually) short sided, seeing only what is near to him, and has become oblivious to the fact that he was cleansed from his old sins......

*" **Because of this, brethren, be all the more solicitous and eager to make sure to ratify, to make steadfast, you're calling and election, for if you do this, you will never stumble or fall.***

Revelation 5:9&10-" You purchased men unto God from every tribe and language and people and nation, and You have made them a kingdom (royal race) and priests to our God, and they shall reign as kings over the earth.